T0161731

Dedicated to my readers

Who need a break from their screens
to live life IRL
And go pursue all their dreams

*Also to my friends, family and dog, Roo B Tuesday

Oh, the Pics That You'll Post!

Maiana Rose

AITIA PRESS • NEW YORK

Congratulations!
Today is the day,
To chase insta-stardom.
And you're ready to SLAY!

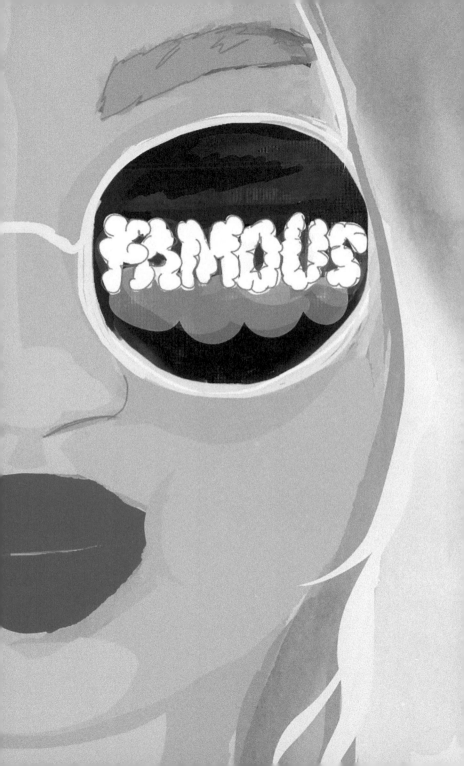

You'll need likes on your posts.
You'll need comments galore,
For a post worthy life,
That ur fans will adore!

You'll follow for follows,
And you'll learn what to tag,
And you'll study the art,
Of the humblest brag…

You will start gaining fans,
And build a brand that will sell!
Aim to make it your job,
Say so long IRL!

Venturing out on your very own feet,
You'll know not to go down,
Any un-trendy street!

So what will u post?
Well, you'll cover all bases,
From the frothiest lattes,
To the hippest shoe laces!

From the #FBFs,
To the #TBTs,
You'll find every occasion,
To update your feed.

You might shop till you drop!

As you max out ur card!

But it's worth looking hip!

Staying on-trend is hard!

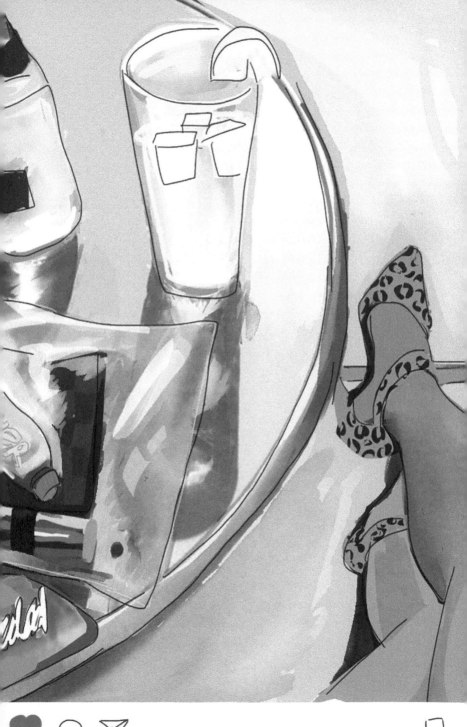

Amidst all the action,
Your page will gain traction,
But still there's more posting to do!

Cus ur follower count
Is but merely a fraction,
Of pets much more trendy than you!

With your cup full of matcha,
  On the hunt for cute eats... 👀

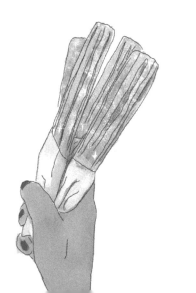

You'll wait hours for ice cream,

Just to hashtag the deets!
@
@

BUT the ice cream might melt,

Before u get the pic right...

So you'll TRY taking selfies
But ya hit some bad light.

And u might second guess,
If you have what it takes.
Since the grammers you idol,
Look so perf, if not FAKE!

Your nose not quite right,
Your brows not on fleek,

Your lips are too small,
Your jawline too weak!

You'll turn on yourself,
For you need to place blame,

What imperfection!
"It's too much" you will claim!

But just in that moment,
Your phone blinks a light,
A follow, a comment, a view, or a like!?

Oh, the pics that you'll post!

And you're back in the game!
A slam dunk with one post...
So continue your journey!
For a life you can boast!

And at times it feels easy,
Other times, yes it's tough...
But if you luck out,
You'll get loads of free stuff!

...But 'til blue marks are checked.
It will not be enough!

So you make it your mission,

To take all the right shots

To cross off your checklist,

Of 'most postworthy' spots!

First start in LA,
You'll post pics with some wings.
Hit the pink wall, of course.
Amongst all of the things...

And what's next on the list,

Well your fans want to know!

That it's festival season!

And you're def gonna go!

Coachella in April,

Burning Man, end of summer...

And IF you don't make it,

That FOMO's a bummer!

Where should you post next?
Well you'll need something soon...
Duh! a tropical, vaycay!
How 'bout Bali AND Tulum!

Yacht rides in Santorini,
It's a tru paradise!
On the official world tour
Of la vida #bestlife!

Your life will be #goalz!
If you make it to Rome,
Much amoré from fans,
You can feel through your phone!

A pitstop in Paris,
Japan, or Phuket?
What a life you will post...
Oh, the places you'll jet!!

Once you arrive,
You'll think it's the end.
You've outdone 'em all
To the far-fetchest trend.

But way up on the moon,

Your phone
has no bars...

Ugh, you can't even post!

ugh

Who will know you're
with stars!?

Now you realize so much,

With perspective from space...

Like, you'll miss out on life,

With a screen in your face!

Instafame has it's perks,

But don't get it all wrong...

There was life before gram...

It's been around for sooo long!

So back "down to earth"

You will go at light speed,

And perhaps u care less,

About posts on your feed....

DOWN TO EARTH

So if once in a while,
You leave your phone behind...
Snap a pic with your heart,
2 upload 2 ur mind!

Glossary 4 Old Folks

- *Bars* - noun, Symbolic graph used to indicate cell phone service strength.

- *Bestlife* - A compound word, specifically invented to describe someone's life when it simply looks perfect based on their social media.

- *Checked blue marks, (i.e.Verified symbol)* - a badge of fame on Instagram.

- *Deets* - noun, Abbreviation for details.

- *Def* - adverb, Abbreviation for definitely: meaning without a doubt!

- *#FBF*- An acronym meaning "Flashback Friday" - used on social media platforms when posting a picture from the past.

- *Feed*- noun, The photos posted by accounts you follow that show up when you are browsing on Instagram.

- *Fleek* - adjective, Trending word for cool. The phrase phrase "on fleek" is synonymous with en vogue.

- *Follows/(to) Follow*- noun & verb, People, or fans, who "follow" your account on Instagram, thus "follows" can refer to the collective number of followers.

- *Fomo* - Acronym meaning Fear Of Missing Out: the opposite of JOMO (Joy Of Missing Out).

- *Goalz* - A dream situation.

- *Gram* - noun & verb, Abbreviation for Instagram. Used as a verb, it is synonymous with "post."

- *Hashtag* - noun, A # symbol in front of a word to associate it with other photos based on a descriptive hashtag. Used to increase popularity of a post.

- *Humble Brag* - Demonstrating how cool your life is, while trying to appear humble.

- *Influencer* - noun, Instagram users with (tens or hundreds of) thousands, even millions of followers, who influence consumer behavior, are frequently sponsored by brands.

- *Insta* - noun & adjective, Abbreviation for Instagram, also a prefix added to any word to make it Instagram related (e.g "instamodel" or "instafamous").

- *Irl* - Acronym for "In Real Life."

- *Likes/ to like* - noun & verb, A form of affection given out on Instagram, signified as a heart; thus to show affection on the platform.

- *Perf* - adjective, Abbreviation for perfect.

- *Pic*- noun, Abbreviation for picture.

- *Pink Wall (the)* - Iconic location for posting, which is located at 8221 Melrose Ave, Los Angeles, CA 90046.

- *Post*- noun & verb To send out an image or message on social media; thus the image or message itself.

- *Slay* - informal, verb, To greatly impress others as being cool or awesome or to totally dominate a situation.

- *Selfie* - noun, Self portrait taken with a cell phone camera.

- *Tag* - noun & verb, To identify a person, place or product on a post, or the identification of a person, place or post.

- *#TBT* - An acronym meaning "Throwback Thursday" - used on social media platforms when posting a picture from the past.

- *Trend/ing* - noun, verb & adjective, What is most currently in the zeitgeist. It spreads like wildfire, thanks to algorithms on social media.

- *Vaycay*- noun & verb, Abbreviation for vacation.

The End

About the Author

East Coast Born, Maiana Rose grew up in Santa Fe, New Mexico, where she attended high school at Santa Fe Preparatory school. She went on to attend Pitzer College, of the Claremont colleges, graduating in 2014 with a BA in interdisciplinary media studies, fine arts, and anthropology. After which, she moved to Los Angeles to pursue a career in entertainment and art. Maiana found an avenue to meld her love of comedy and art when she decided to start an illustrated Instagram account from which she lovingly mocks social media trends. Also, she attempts to bring to light some issues society faces surrounding social media, mostly, the amount of importance people place on it. Maiana sees *Oh, the Pics That You'll Post!* as a way to poke light fun at ourselves, while also sending a message to the up and coming generations that Instagram and other social media platforms are not "life." Out of her illustrated series, she began a line of postcards which she sold to local retailers around Los Angeles, then moved on, to begin her career as an author, putting out her first book, *Oh, the Pics That You'll Post!* and hopes to continue authoring and illustrating books with a little edge of social commentary and humor.

More information about Maiana and news about her art can be found at www.drawlaland.com.

If you feel so inspired…
You can make your own rhyme…
And please share it with me
If you find the time!

_____

_____

_____

_____

_____

_____

_____

_____

_____

_____

_____

_____

_____

_____

_____

_____

_____

_____

_____

Slide into my DM's @Drawlaland
Tweet @Drawlaland

A free ebook edition
is available with the
purchase of this book.

To claim your free ebook edition:

1. Visit MorganJamesBOGO.com
2. Sign your name CLEARLY in the space
3. Complete the form and submit a photo of the entire copyright page
4. You or your friend can download the ebook to your preferred device

Print & Digital Together Forever.

Snap a photo

Free ebook

Read anywhere